The Key To The SUPERNATURAL

Kenneth Hagin Jr.

The Key To The SUPERNATURAL

By Kenneth Hagin Jr.

The Lord has been showing me for some time now that the key to the last-day move of the supernatural power of God will be found in two words: "unity" and "accord."

According to the dictionary, the word *"unity"* means "the state of being one or united; oneness; singleness." Another definition is "the quality of being one in spirit, sentiment, purpose, etc." Unity also "implies oneness, as in spirit, aims, interests, feelings, etc., of that which is made up of diverse elements or individuals."

"*Accord*" means almost the same thing: "to make, agree or harmonize; to be in agreement or harmony; mutual agreement; harmony; all agreeing; with no one dissenting."

The Theme of Acts

If you have ever studied Bible history, you will know that unity (or accord) actually is the theme of the Book of Acts. The word "accord," for example, is found 11 times in this book: Acts 1:14, 2:1, 2:46, 4:24, 5:12, 7:57, 8:6, 12:20, 15:25, 18:12, and 19:29.

In the King James Version, the words "unity" and "accord" are used interchangeably. The meaning of "accord" in the following verses from Acts is "being one in spirit, purpose, aim, and so forth."

ACTS 1:14

14 These all continued WITH ONE ACCORD in prayer and supplication . . . .

ACTS 2:1

1 And when the day of Pentecost was fully come, they were all WITH ONE ACCORD in one place.

ACTS 2:46

46 And they, continuing daily WITH ONE ACCORD in the temple, and breaking bread from house to house, did eat their meat with gladness, and singleness of heart . . . .

ACTS 4:24

24 And when they heard that, they lifted up their voice to God WITH ONE ACCORD . . . .

ACTS 5:12

12 And by the hands of the apostles were many signs and wonders wrought among the people; (and they were all WITH ONE ACCORD in Solomon's porch.

ACTS 8:6

6 And the people WITH ONE ACCORD gave heed unto those things which Philip spake, hearing and seeing the miracles which he did.

ACTS 12:20
20 And Herod was highly displeased with them
of Tyre and Sidon: but they came WITH ONE
ACCORD to him . . . .

ACTS 15:25
25 It seemed good unto us, being assembled
WITH ONE ACCORD, to send chosen men unto
you with our beloved Barnabas and Paul.

(The same concept is found in Romans
15:6: *"That ye may with **one mind** and **one
mouth** glorify God, even the Father of our
Lord Jesus Christ."*)

Unity in the Early Church

Tremendous things happened in the
Book of Acts. Let's study these Scriptures.

In Acts 1, we see the New Testament
believers continuing "with one accord" in
prayer and supplication.

In Acts 2 we find them worshipping
daily "with one accord" in the Temple and

eating their meals with gladness and "singleness of heart."

In the third chapter of Acts, we see Peter and John healing a crippled man at the Gate Beautiful. The people rejoiced, but the religious leaders got upset and called the two apostles before the Sanhedrin.

When these rulers of the people and elders of Israel heard Peter and John, they marveled: *"Now when they saw the boldness of Peter and John, and perceived that they were unlearned and ignorant men, they marvelled; and they took knowledge of them, that they had been with Jesus"* (Acts 4:13).

Because all of the people were for Peter and John, the leaders were afraid to do anything to them. They threatened them and let them go. The fourth chapter of Acts records the mighty prayer meeting the believers held.

ACTS 4:23,24,29-32

23 And being let go, they went to their own company, and reported all that the chief priests and elders had said unto them.

24 And when they heard that, they lifted up their voice to God WITH ONE ACCORD, and said, Lord, thou art God, which hast made heaven, and earth, and the sea . . . .

29 And now, Lord, behold their threatenings: and grant unto thy servants, that with all boldness they may speak thy word,

30 By stretching forth thine hand to heal; and that signs and wonders may be done by the name of thy holy child Jesus.

31 And when they had prayed, the place was shaken where they were assembled together; and they were all filled with the Holy Ghost, and they spake the word of God with boldness.

32 And the multitude of them that believed were of one heart and of one soul . . . .

Did those believers get down and pray, "And now, Lord, behold their threatenings: and grant unto thy servants grace to endure the persecution and hardships. Grant that we can hold out faithful to the end"? Is that what your Bible says? No, that's not what it says.

Look closely at these verses. Grasp the concepts of "unity" and "accord" expressed here. There could have been more than 3,000 praying here. It wasn't just the two apostles praying; it was the whole company of believers in Jerusalem.

We know that 120 persons were assembled on the Day of Pentecost, and 3,000 more came to the Lord after Peter preached his message that day. That makes 3,120 believers. There may have been still more in the company who had accepted the Lord after witnessing the healing of the crippled man, because Acts 4:21 says, *"all men glorified God for that which was done."*

The rulers had warned Peter and John not to speak *"in that name."* (They couldn't bring themselves even to say the Name of Jesus.) But in verse 30 we see the believers praying *"by **the name of** thy holy child **Jesus**."*

Unity: The Key to the Supernatural

Verse 31 is the one I like: *"the place was shaken where they were assembled together."*

When we in the Body of Christ begin to unite ourselves in the unity and power of the Word of God, we're going to see some places shaken as they never have been shaken before. The reason the supernatural power of God has not been demonstrated as God would have liked in years gone by is because believers got in unity only at sporadic times.

I believe in this last day before Jesus Christ comes again there is going to come a unity among the Body of Christ that the world has never seen before, and the power of God is going to be demonstrated as never before!

Somebody asked me, "Ken, why did we see such a move of the supernatural power of God the last week of July at the Tulsa Campmeeting '78?"

I replied, "I don't really know for sure, but I have some ideas." That was when God began to deal with me about unity.

Every night of Campmeeting there were at least 10,000 people in the Tulsa Assembly Center, because that is what it seats, and it was full. Those people were bound together in singleness of mind upon the Word of God. Not upon emotionalism. Not upon sensationalism. Not upon some human personality.

And when that many people get together in unity and power, God Almighty overcomes every obstacle and demonstrates His supernatural power!

The four ministries that cooperated in the Campmeeting—the Kenneth Hagin,

Kenneth Copeland, John Osteen, and Fred Price ministries—were in unity and accord. They were not there to lift up any man.

Although we are diverse individuals from diverse backgrounds, and although we have different names over our ministries, we must come into this kind of unity and harmony.

As long as basic doctrine is based on the Word of God, we must recognize the whole Body of Christ, even though we do not see eye-to-eye with all groups on petty idiosyncrasies.

(Some of the men may not wear their hair short enough for you. They may wear flashy suits. Some of the women may put on makeup. You think they should wear *short* hair, *drab* suits, and *no* makeup. That's what I mean when I talk about little idiosyncrasies.)

Laborers Together

We need to forget these incidentals and unite ourselves on the Word of God to fight this last-day onslaught of the enemy. Satan is going to bring every power from the depths of hell against God's people and all humanity in these last days. The Word of God says he has come *"to steal, and to kill, and to destroy"* (John 10:10). Satan knows his time is short, and he's going to give it everything he's got.

As we band together, however, in the unity of the Word of God, the Body of Christ will rise in triumphant power over Satan—*because he already has been defeated!*

One person may say, "Oh, I'm a follower of Hagin." Another may say, "I sort of follow Copeland." Still another may say, "I like this one or that one."

That reminds me of what the Apostle

Paul wrote in First Corinthians 3:

1 CORINTHIANS 3:3-9

3 For ye are yet carnal: for whereas there is among you envying, and strife, and divisions, are ye not carnal, and walk as men?

4 For while one saith, I am of Paul; and another, I am of Apollos; are ye not carnal?

5 Who then is Paul, and who is Apollos, but ministers by whom ye believed, even as the Lord gave to every man?

6 I have planted, Apollos watered; but God gave the increase.

7 So then neither is he that planteth any thing, neither he that watereth; but God that giveth the increase.

8 Now he that planteth and he that watereth are one: and every man shall receive his own reward according to his own labour.

9 For we are labourers together with God: ye are God's husbandry, ye are God's building.

The Lord Is Your Shepherd

Paul is saying, "It doesn't matter *who*

brought you the Gospel as long as you were saved by the blood, power, and Lordship of the Lord Jesus Christ.''

No matter who brought you into the faith—Kenneth Hagin, your pastor, or some other minister—you are not following a man. You are not following man's doctrine. You are following the Word of God—the doctrine of the Lord Jesus Christ.

Paul also said, *"But though we, or an angel from heaven, preach any other gospel unto you than that which we have preached unto you, let him be accursed"* (Gal. 1:8). Notice that Paul even includes himself in that statement.

Too many people have things out of perspective. They have taken a revelation God gave to one man, grabbed a portion of it, ran off, and perverted it. Forget about human personalities and lift up the Word!

Jesus said, *"And I, if I be lifted up from*

the earth, will draw all men unto me" (John 12:32.) Not if Kenneth Hagin is lifted up. Not if you are lifted up. But if Jesus Christ is lifted up. That is part of the unity we must come into.

We must forget about our own ministries and fellowships. We must forget about who we are and what we want to be. We must unite ourselves around the Word of God. As we do, we will see ourselves ushered into an age of the supernatural power of God. Jesus promised:

JOHN 14:12
12 Verily, verily, I say unto you, He that believeth on me, the works that I do shall he do also; and GREATER WORKS than these shall he do; because I go unto my Father.

We have yet to see all these *greater works* be accomplished, because the Church of the Lord Jesus Christ has failed to unite, and therefore the power of God has been unable to move.

Where there is unity, every gift of the Spirit and every fruit of the spirit will be in operation. Then and only then can the supernatural power of God move.

Do you know why most people are not in unity and harmony? Because they don't have enough of the Word of God—enough power—in them. How can the gifts of the Spirit or the fruit of the spirit operate in them?

Too many Christians have forgotten Galatians 5:22,23, where the fruit of the spirit is listed: love, joy, peace, long-suffering, gentleness, goodness, faith, meekness, and temperance. All of these need to be in demonstration.

Spiritual Discipline

A lot of people want to talk about faith. They want to talk about their confession and what they can have through their confession. However, they do not want you to talk to them about the fruit of the spirit. They do not want you to talk to them about being meek or patient. They *especially* do not want you to talk to them about love, because love carries many connotations — and one of the connotations love carries is discipline.

Hear me, Body of Christ: One of the connotations love carries is discipline! People don't like to hear that word. If you come to RHEMA Bible Training Center, the first thing you will hear me teach in Practical Ministries is, "To be successful in the ministry, you must learn to discipline yourself in the spiritual realm the way you do in the natural."

I am not talking about being disciplined according to somebody's theological idea. I am not talking about being disciplined according to somebody's constitution and bylaws. I am talking about being disciplined according to the Word of God.

I think it's time we quit having spiritual taffy thrown into the lap of an already diabetic congregation.

I think it's time preachers reached down into the Word of God and began to dish out what the Word has to say, because we have come to the time the Apostle Paul was telling Timothy about:

2 TIMOTHY 4:3,4
3 For the time will come when they will not endure sound doctrine; but after their own lusts shall they heap to themselves teachers, having itching ears;
4 And they shall turn away their ears from the truth, and shall be turned unto fables.

I think it's time we come into the unity of the Word of God concerning salvation, the Holy Spirit, healing, faith, operation of the gifts of the Spirit, the fruit of the spirit, biblical theology, and many other things.

A lot of people are talking about the

Holy Spirit these days, but I've got news for you: There are a lot more people *talking* about the Holy Spirit than have actually *experienced* the infilling of the Holy Spirit.

When you are truly born again, there is a change in your life. Similarly, when you truly experience the infilling of the Holy Spirit, there is a change in your life. Holy boldness and the supernatural power of God become resident, and they are quickly discerned by the spiritually aware.

Strife in Worship

Another area where unity is needed is the area of worship. If we are to have the power to do the *greater works* Jesus promised, we must unify ourselves in worship. Charismatics and other church people have had great problems in this area.

One of the reasons the supernatural

power of God has been hampered is because there is strife in worship. The devil is subtle and cunning. It goes back to the verse that says, *"the little foxes* (little things) ... *spoil the vines...."* (Song of Solomon 2:15).

Churches, fellowships, prayer groups — whatever you want to call them—are too quick to criticize fellow believers. Perhaps one group jumps and hollers in its worship. People in another group across town just raise their hands and quietly worship. Those in the first group think the second should be just like them. And the quiet ones are quick to criticize the whoopers and hollerers. That's strife. That's not unity. How can you expect the power of God to operate at its *fullest* in these conditions?

Then one church does something another doesn't approve of. One church, strong in faith, believes God to supply all its needs. The other church is not quite up to that level of faith yet so it holds a rummage or bake sale. Those in the first church are quick to say, "Bless God, if you had *faith*, you wouldn't have to have one of those sales!"

Yes, bless God, but if you've ever read the Apostle Paul, you would know he said, "If you are strong in faith, don't criticize the one who is weaker in faith." There is no unity or harmony where the strong in faith are criticizing the weak in faith.

Those strong in faith should be willing to condescend to fellowship with the others. They should worship with them, even if it goes across their grain sometimes. They should work with them until they can raise them to their own level of faith. Then they will see the supernatural power of God in demonstration.

When my dad was pastoring a certain church many years ago, he couldn't get one of his Sunday School teachers to believe for her healing. She was scheduled for surgery.

Finally Dad said to her, "Listen, what *can* you believe for?"

She answered, "I can believe that the operation will be a success. I can believe for a miraculously quick recovery."

He said, "Okay. Now I've got *something.*" He came down from his high level of faith when he realized he couldn't raise her level of faith any. He didn't criticize her. He found out on which level he could agree with her, and then he agreed with her.

You might say, "You mean that man of faith went down there and agreed with her that the doctors would perform a perfect operation and that her recovery would be miraculous?"

Yes, he did. According to the prayer of agreement, he put his faith with hers.

She went to the hospital and had the operation. At that time, years and years ago, the doctors did not have all the technology we have today, and her operation was considered major surgery.

Afterwards the doctor insisted she have a shot for pain, even though she was in no pain. That's the only medication she needed. She was up and out of that hospital in no time. Miraculous! They got what they believed for.

It wasn't long until Dad was able to increase her faith so that she could believe God for more. Finally he had her to the point that every time there was a problem in her life, she used her faith. She did not need to go back for any more operations.

That was unity in practice.

Application to Spiritual Life

Now let's bring it over and apply it to

the spiritual life. Unity is the only thing that will work if you want to see the power of God and the "greater works."

Pastors, don't be afraid you will lose some of your church members to another church if you cooperate with them. Don't be afraid you will lose some of your prayer group if you begin to fellowship with another group.

Get interested in building the Kingdom of God and not your own little kingdom, and you will find that things will work out much better for you. You see, too many ministers have this backwards. Each is interested in building only his own ministry.

That's one thing reporters from the Tulsa newspapers can't understand about my father at our annual Campmeeting, which attracts thousands of people to Tulsa. Dad sits down and lets other ministers get up and speak in his services. The reporters just can't understand that kind of unselfishness.

When we are working together in love and unity, we will prefer one another. We will not be interested in building our own ministries. We will be interested only in building the Kingdom of God.

It says in Psalm 75:6,7, *"Promotion cometh neither from the east, nor from the west, nor from the south. But God is the judge: he putteth down one, and setteth up another."* If you do your part in building the Kingdom, God will promote you. If you are worried about getting yourself promoted and are busy trying to get recognition for what you have done, forget about getting promoted.

If you want to get recognized, get on your knees and pray. Always be full of love and full of the Word of God. Be available to help when something needs to be done around the church. It won't be long until you will be recognized from the platform.

Some people just can't realize that if they would get into the Word and be faithful where God has them, they would be ready to be promoted when the proper time came.

The Apostle Paul continually warned us about giving more importance to ourselves than we should. He continually stressed the need for unity.

Where there is no unity, strife comes in. Then division. Then faith quits working. And when faith quits working, sickness comes in, financial disaster appears, spiritual stagnation sets in, and everything becomes a mess. Simply because somebody thought more highly of himself than he should have.

You and I have the greatest opportunity of any generation that has ever lived; greater even than the work the apostles faced. Our opportunity includes binding ourselves together to go into a world hoodwinked by theologians, churchized, revivalized, and torn apart by the devil until it has become a religious mess.

I walk into some churches and shake my head. I see a little old-time Pentecostalism. I see some modern liberal theology. I even have seen a little of the eastern occult—yes, in so-called charismatic fellowships, getting over into the area of Transcendental Meditation.

How in the world can God move in such places? They have *"a form of godliness, but denying the power thereof"* (2 Tim. 3:5). And that's all they have.

As my father so aptly puts it, many of the people who are supposed to know what is going on in the religious world wouldn't know the Holy Spirit if they saw Him coming down the street with a red hat on. That would be funny if it weren't so pathetic.

Unity must—*must*—abound in these

last days if we are to see the supernatural
power of God demonstrated as it is supposed to be.

My End-Time Vision

I look out on the horizon of time, and I
see an opening in the eastern sky. I know
that Jesus Christ is coming.

Then I look on this earth, and I see a
group of people known as the sons of God.

I can see the sword of the Spirit and the
shield of faith in their hands. They are
clothed with truth. Their feet are shod
with the preparation of the Gospel of
peace. They are wearing the helmet of salvation and the breastplate of righteous-
ness.

They not only know how to take the
Word of God and let it be the *logos* to them,
but they also know how to put it in their
spirits, turn it around, and let it become

the *rhema.*

I see them united, standing like soldiers. Then I see them begin to march in unity and harmony, and I see the spoken Word of God—the *rhema*—begin to flow from their mouths.

In my mind's eye I see them marching forth across this land. As the Word comes out of their mouths, I see the Spirit of God confirming it with signs following.

I see the host begin to grow. I see others reach down, pick up a shield of faith to ward off the fiery darts of the enemy, and begin to march.

I see them pick up the distressed and the diseased. I see them pick up those shackled in chains. They become a stronger and stronger body. They march on—right over the top of the devil!

They are walking in love, harmony, and unity, demonstrating all of the fruit of the spirit. *They are marching to meet their*

Lord and Savior who is coming in that eastern sky!

I see the world. Then I see the Body of the Lord Jesus Christ move into the sea. I see it circle the globe and return to its starting place. And as the first ones reach that starting place, I hear in the distance the sound of the trumpet!

I see the clouds begin to open!

I see a Man in white, glistening with all the glory and the power of God, begin to descend!

I see the graves begin to open, and I see the bodies begin to ascend!

Suddenly, I see those first few who were in the battle. Their feet begin to leave the ground!

There's the first row! Now the second row! Now the third! They begin to go up together with the Lord.

YOU SEE, THE UNITY OF BELIEVERS WILL BRING THE

LORD JESUS CHRIST BACK TO THIS EARTH!

Hastening the Lord's Return

We say, "Oh, I want to see Him." We sing, "I want to stroll over heaven ...." If we really want to hasten the coming of the Lord Jesus Christ, we will forget the diversities of the past, unite together around the Word of God, and deliver the world from the chains that bind it.

That is where we are today. For the salvation and deliverance of this world, it will take all of us—and more—bound together in unity, letting the mind of Christ dwell in us. Jesus was not double-minded. He had one purpose: to set the world free. That is our purpose. That is our aim.

Our formula for success is found in

Philippians chapter 2:

PHILIPPIANS 2:1-5
1 If there be therefore any consolation in Christ, if any comfort of love, if any fellowship of the Spirit, if any bowels and mercies,
2 Fulfil ye my joy, that ye be likeminded, having the same love, being of ONE ACCORD, of ONE MIND.
3 Let nothing be done through strife or vainglory; but in lowliness of mind let each esteem other better than themselves.
4 Look not every man on his own things, but every man also on the things of others.
5 Let this mind be in you, which was also in Christ Jesus.

This is the message of the hour: *Unite. Unite in God's Word to see the power of God prevail.*